Heartfelt
MOMENTS

Heartfelt MOMENTS

TREASURES OF THE HEART

DERRICK GRAHAM

iUniverse

HEARTFELT MOMENTS
TREASURES OF THE HEART

iUniverse books may be ordered through booksellers or by contacting:

iUniverse
1663 Liberty Drive
Bloomington, IN 47403
www.iuniverse.com
1-800-Authors (1-800-288-4677)

Because of the dynamic nature of the Internet, any web addresses or links contained in this book may have changed since publication and may no longer be valid. The views expressed in this work are solely those of the author and do not necessarily reflect the views of the publisher, and the publisher hereby disclaims any responsibility for them.

Any people depicted in stock imagery provided by Thinkstock are models, and such images are being used for illustrative purposes only. Certain stock imagery © Thinkstock.

ISBN: 978-1-5320-0814-6 (sc)
ISBN: 978-1-5320-0815-3 (e)

Library of Congress Control Number: 2016915972

Print information available on the last page.

iUniverse rev. date: 10/19/2016

ACKNOWLEDGEMENTS

I would like to first thank my almighty Savior Jesus Christ for giving this gift to share with the world. And to my lovely wife, Felesha, for supporting me through this entire project. You have inspired me to do great things and I thank the Lord every day for your love and dedication.

ACKNOWLEDGEMENTS

CONTENTS

SPIRITUAL

Having Faith 1

Church.. 3

God's Angels 5

Stepping Out on Faith.. 7

His Love.. 9

MILITARY

Our Soldiers.. 11

Our Flag.. 13

Happy Father's Day.. 15

Independence Day 17

Fallen Heroes 19

SENSUAL

My Desire 21

My Description of You 23

You Are 25

Hand and Hand.. 27

Joyful 29

Someone Special.. 31

Once in a Lifetime 33

GENERAL

A Bad Day..35

A Cup of Coffee...37

A Winter Storm, Part I...39

Adolescent Years..41

Life's Encounters...43

Childhood Memories...45

Faces in the Sky...47

Heartfelt Moments..49

A Mother's Love..51

I Have No Time for This..53

Incarcerated...55

Left All Alone..57

Life's Questions...59

Paper and Ink..61

The Puzzle of Life...63

Tread Softly..65

Dear Son..67

A Father's Love..69

Dear Brother..71

What I See..73

Mom...75

INSPIRATIONAL

Why I Love to Write..77

A Strong Woman...79

A World in Crisis...81

Because of You...83

Big Brother/Big Sister...85

Having Endurance...87

Remember Me..89

Survival...91

My Greatest Moment 93

A Woman's Unconditional Love 95

Foundation of Life 97

In the Name of Love 99

Painful Moments... 101

Life Experiences 103

Emotions.. 105

My Gift 107

Dear Dad 109

Treasures of the Heart.. 111

Deeply Thinking 113

Having Faith

Since you have opened this book,
Please understand my position,
Since God has entered my life,
I've been going through a transition.
And through these experiences,
Life seemed to be unfair,
I didn't acknowledge the problem,
Nor did I really care.
So instead of telling you,
I wanted to share my thoughts,
About some of the anomalies,
And the battles that I've fought.
I believe that was the problem,
I really couldn't see,
Instead of holding on to faith,
I was only thinking of me.
So as you continue to read,
I've learned something too,
We all have these trials,
That must go through.

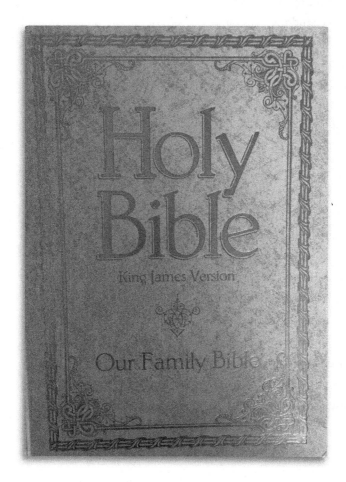

Church

As I sat in the congregation, listening to each word
As the pastor delivered the message, recalling what I heard
I sat there for a minute, listen intently to what was said
I allowed the words to sink, deeply inside my head
Then I asked myself, how could this be?
He died upon the cross, just to save me?
As I continued to listen, about the things He has done
He did it not only for me, but He did it for everyone
As I was in deep thought, I looked around the place
I saw there was a tear, falling from every face
My heart felt overjoyed, for embracing His love
Now I know the feeling, which everyone's been speaking of
And when I left that morning, and began driving home
I began to feel special, to know that I wasn't alone
He has always comforted me, no matter what I've done
I know His love is a blessing, for each and everyone
So if I have transgressed, please forgive me
I will be a better man, that's what I want to be
So please have some patience, it may take some time
As He begins to transform, my body, heart, and mind

God's Angels

I've always felt strong, when I was around you
You gave me the confidence, which I never knew
You've showed me so much, in such a short time
I hold on to those memories, because they're all mine
I've found myself dreaming, and often thinking of you
Wanting a second chance, so I could talk to you
There are so many things, which I didn't get to say
I made plans to tell you, but you suddenly passed away
As my heart began to mourn, and tears fell from my eyes
The news of your passing, took me by surprise
It hurt me so much; I didn't know what to do
All I could think of, was me being without you
The thought hurt me more, than words could ever say
I knew you wouldn't want me, to be acting this way
I needed to regain my composure, and continue to move
Because I know that's, what you would want me to do
When I think of the good times, I will always cherish that
When God gives us angels, He's going to want them back

Stepping Out on Faith

When I'm feeling down, I ask what can I do
Lord, in order for me, to get a little closer to you
How can I be worthy? Of all of your good deeds
When all I have is faith, the size of a mustard seed
How can I be happy? When troubles get in my way?
How can I be strong? When I have a bad day?
When I think of everything, that you have done for me
Like being my eyes, when I could not see
Or when I felt neglected, and so desperately alone
It was you who comforted me, when I was on my own
You have done so much, and shown me another way
That I must step out on faith, no matter what people say

His Love

My spirituality comforts me,
It allows me to have a link,
During good and bad times,
It guides my soul as I think.
My divinity is so precious,
It means more to me each day,
It helps me step out on faith,
No matter what they may say.
My salvation is a blessing,
It has been bestowed unto me,
Reminding me of His love,
And what He's done for me.

Our Soldiers

For all the sacrifices you have made,
It was a difficult thing to do,
For all the long deployments,
It was something you had to do.
For all of the letters,
I received along the way,
The words meant so much,
I thought of you each day.
For all the times you spent,
For making our world so safe,
For all the precautions you took,
To make this a better place.
For all the restless nights,
You all stayed on alert,
For all the relentless bombs,
That landed in the dirt.
For all the scary moments,
For placing yourself in harm's way,
For you loyalty and dedication,
And all the nights you prayed.
For all the holidays that came by,
And for those you didn't see,
Because you were on the battlefield,
Protecting the world for me.
You all will never be forgotten,
I wish I could give you more,
But all I have is these words,
And this is what I thank you for.

Our Flag

Old Glory has been around,
And witnessed many things,
She has flown over our country,
As the war bell rings.
She was in Japan,
As the troops raised her high,
To symbolize our presence,
Our commitment will never die.
She has been laid over,
Our fallen soldiers each year,
We thank you for your service,
Your sacrifice of blood and tears.
She represents our country,
The land of the free,
As we come together,
Illustrating our country's unity.

Happy Father's Day

Happy Father's Day to all,
I want to say this to you,
For the all the special things,
That you have been able to do.
For those whom are at work,
And can't seem to enjoy the day,
Because of other obligations,
We still thank you anyway.
For those that are deployed,
And sailing across the sea,
We haven't forgotten about you,
Happy Father's Day to you from me.
For those overseas,
And working in foreign lands,
To those that are on the beaches,
Protecting our shores across sand.
And for those single mothers,
To you I must say,
Who have raised their children alone?
To you Happy Father's Day.

Independence Day

Through all their preparation,
Through all their sweat and tears,
Through their final hours,
Through their greatest fears.
They have faced many enemies,
In which they've paid the price,
To fight for our freedom,
An unselfish sacrifice.
As we reflect on those times,
On what they did that day,
There aren't enough words,
That can express what I must say.
This is the greatest country,
That will ever be,
Because of what those fallen soldiers,
Did for you and me.
So as we give thanks,
Let's hold our heads up high,
Place your hand over your heart,
As Old Glory continues to fly.
We commemorate you all,
By thanking you today,
For our independence,
On this special day.

Fallen Heroes

The plane has landed,
Underneath the rollers come out,
Old Glory is covering the caskets,
As many scream and shout.
Their hands cover their faces,
The tears begin to flow,
Their hearts full of sorrow,
As the horn continues to blow.
Soldiers begin to march,
With precision and in tune,
The fallen have returned,
They will be put to rest soon.
Everyone was being comforted,
By their family and their friends,
To bring to closure the life,
Of a fallen hero once again.

My Desire

Your body is so erotic,
Your skin is so smooth,
Your perfume is so pleasurable,
I'm so attracted to you.
My composure is weakened,
My mind losses control,
Your love is demanding,
Your thoughts touch my soul.
We embrace with a hug,
Then an intimate kiss,
I've never felt this before,
I couldn't imagine this.
My hands at your waist,
Pulling you closer to me,
I have a surprise for you,
But what could it be.
We go to the bedroom,
And slowly close the door,
Just think for yourself,
That's what imagination is for?

My Description of You

She has light colored eyes, and a pair of gorgeous lips
A very small waist, which compliments her hips
Her walk is so seductive; her presence is full of grace
Her fragrance fills the room, I'm just longing for a taste
Her chest is voluptuous, and so perfectly round
Her body is so sensual, communicating with no sound
We're speaking the same language, now it's obvious to me
That my insatiable appetite, is getting the best of me
I quickly loosen my tie, while I'm trying to think
"Scotch on the rocks", I said, I definitely need a drink
The bartender gave me the drink, and then another shot
I drank both of them fast, they made my chest hot
It was difficult for me, I need to regain control
But it's much too late; she's already tainted my soul

You Are

You are my smile, each day
You make me happy, more than I can say
You make me strong, to make it through
And I thank the Lord, for creating you
You are my life, which has no end
You are my ally, much more than a friend
You are so precious, for the world to see
I'm thankful for this gift, which has been given to me

Hand and Hand

We were on the beach,
Walking hand and hand,
The further that we walked,
There more footprints were in the sand.
As we turned around,
It was obvious to see,
There were two sets of prints,
Caused by you and me.
Then the water washed up,
Onto the sandy shore,
It was so cool and refreshing,
A feeling I adored.
As we kept on walking,
You held on to my hand,
An unbreakable union,
Formed by woman and man.
When we reached our destination,
I turned around to see,
The footprints were still there,
Caused by you and me.

Joyful

Relationships are wonderful,
A beautiful bond that's shared,
By two loving people,
Devoted and who always care.
They will stand side by side,
Through the toughest of times,
Remembering those special vows,
To love each other so kind.
But when things get touch,
You know what they'll do,
Hold on to each other,
Just as often lovers do.
When one of them becomes sick,
And not their best one day,
The other one becomes much stronger,
To carry them the rest of the way.
And from this small token,
What I really want you to see,
How much I do love you,
That's how much you mean to me.

Someone Special

To have someone so special,
Is a blessing in disguise?
Often times you don't see it,
When it's in front of your eyes.
To have someone to love,
Is a blessing so true?
A strong bonded relationship,
With a confirmation of two.
To have someone to trust,
Requires a lot of time,
To solidify the relationship,
With your heart and mind.
To have someone so special,
Is a blessing for two?
And that's what I've found,
By being with you.

Once in a Lifetime

I've waited for so long,
To have someone like you,
Someone full of life,
That would love me too.
Even though times get rough,
And I've been stressed some days,
You've always stayed committed,
And still love me the same.
You never acknowledged my flaws,
But somehow you knew,
You didn't hold that against me
You always remain true.
You never asked for much,
You were just happy and content,
With what I could give you,
Which were the special times we spent?
My offering wasn't monetary,
But something much more,
Than I had ever given anyone,
In my life before.
That is commitment and devotion,
Intangibles you can't see,
This is why I'm offering you,
Every loving part of me.

A Bad Day

Collectively I've gathered my thoughts,
To organize in a certain way,
I don't want any confusion,
In what I'm about to say.
I want people to listen to me,
I want them to hear me clear,
I don't want anyone to misinterpret,
What they're about to hear.
I am confident in my ability,
To do what I do each day,
I am competent enough,
To understand what you say.
When you're having a bad day,
Be mindful of what you do,
You might not be the only one,
That's having a bad day too.
I've seen it many times,
Relationships have been lost,
When you act out on emotions,
You have to pay the cost.
This is just a reminder,
When you're having a bad day,
Make sure you are careful,
About the words you say.

A Cup of Coffee

As the sun arises,
A beautiful sight to see,
There aren't any distractions,
Interrupting this moment for me.
Many different colors,
Cover the once blue sky,
The birds begin to chirp,
As they continue to fly by.
The temperature is comfortable,
Coupled with a gentle breeze,
As I sit on the porch,
Enjoying a cup of coffee.
The sun begins to rise higher,
The heat begins to climb,
I've just finished my first cup,
It's time to go inside.
I'm looking outside,
As I close the door,
This is the greatest moment,
That I often look for.
Such a peaceful morning,
This is how it should be,
Each time I awake,
A perfect morning for coffee.

A Winter Storm, Part I

Looking off in the distance,
Beyond the trees and the snow,
In the warmth of a log cabin,
Staring out the window.
The fireplace is burning,
It's a little past noon,
Anticipating a winter storm,
That will be there soon.
On the stove there's a pot,
Of coffee freshly brewed,
There's a cup on the table,
And a plate of eaten food.
In the living room on the floor,
There's a newly authentic rug,
Where man's best friend resides,
All peacefully and snugged.
On the table in the room,
An old ash tray sits,
A half smoked cigar,
On the edge still lit.
He leaves the foggy window,
And enters the room,
And sits in his favorite chair,
The storm will there soon.

Adolescent Years

When I was a teenager,
My emotions began to change,
It felt so different,
I thought it was so strange.
I needed to talk to someone,
Who has experienced this before?
I didn't know who to ask,
Even I wasn't too sure.
I wanted to ask my friends,
Someone close to my age,
It was too difficult to discuss,
I thought it was too strange.
But then I stopped to think,
And recalled on all those times,
My teenage years are now memories
Stored inside my mind.

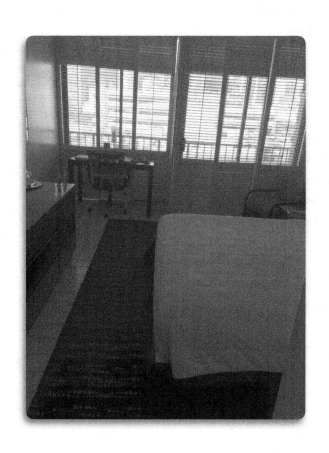

Life's Encounters

Feelings are strong emotions, often times we ignore
They make us act out of character, something we shouldn't ignore
At times it's hard to control, when compulsive thoughts collide
You attempt to remain calm, by holding it inside
As it continues to escalate, you're slowly losing control
You can feel the anger, just waiting to explode
It becomes so chaotic, thoughts racing through your head
Becoming angrier, listening to what was said
As you turn to walk away, and try to calm down
You just want to meditate, without hearing a sound
You go to the other room, and lie on the bed
You mind begins to think, about the hurtful things were said
As you stare at the ceiling, you know you need some time
To completely calm down, and settle your mind

Childhood Memories

When I was a child,
I remembered having a lot fun,
Especially during the summertime,
Playing with everyone.
We use to eat ice cream,
To beat the summer heat,
It seemed to be too much,
Radiating off the concrete.
That still didn't stop us,
We would continue to play,
Thinking of something to do,
Differently the next day.
Then something happened,
There was a familiar sound,
The delicious smell of popcorn,
The carnival had come to town.
We were so excited,
This is all we could think of,
A large children's playground,
I think that I'm in love.
When it was all over,
The rides were taken down,
I can say I had so much fun,
Because the carnival came to town.

Faces in the Sky

As I look into the sky,
The clouds form faces,
But I don't know why.
Is it just me?
Or my train of thought,
Is it a picture?
In which my eyes just caught,
Is it a face?
In which I long to see,
Of someone so strong,
And dear to me.
Is it just something,
That was said,
That conjured this image,
Inside my head.
I have many questions,
But no answers for me,
That would help me solve,
This intriguing mystery.

Heartfelt Moments

There are so many moments,
I will cherish in my lifetime,
A lot of childhood memories,
Resonate within my mind.
Most of them are heartfelt,
Some painful I couldn't see,
Others had a tremendous impact,
This was difficult for me.
As I begin to think back,
On some of those childhood days,
I acknowledged what I've done,
And the bad choices that I made.
It helped me to understand,
The things that I've done wrong,
It allowed me to grow to up,
Accept responsibility to move on.
The past is not meant to last,
It's just a thought in time,
Referencing my heartfelt moments,
Only inside my mind.

A Mother's Love

I've watched you struggle, through so many years
As a little boy, I didn't understand your tears
When we were in church, and I often saw you cry
I watched your behavior, but didn't understand why
And when I got sick, you held me so tight
And kept a watchful eye, over me throughout the night
When I didn't tell the truth, you would discipline me
I was so angry, for what you did to me
And when I wanted to leave, you would tell me no
I felt I couldn't do anything, because you wouldn't let me go
So as I got older, and I was no longer a kid
I wanted to know why; you did the things you did
I guess I would never understand, the things that you do
Because if I was in your position, I wouldn't do the same to you

I Have No Time for This

You think that it's easy,
To wipe my tears away,
After all that you've done,
And the terrible things you say.
I guess it's out of anger,
Or malice from your heart,
This is the main reason,
Why we fell apart.
Having these childish tantrums,
Only proves to me,
That you haven't grown up,
This is what I believe.
You think I have no feelings,
Because they don't always show,
But I'm better than that,
And this you already know.

Mimi Miller
0123 Never forget me
Stay Strong TI 2172

Sally Wells 1209160
Toney City Correctional facility
Everyone Needs Mail
29164

Incarcerated

He looks at himself in the mirror,
Wondering why he's so alone,
Being locked inside this cage,
When he should be at home.
He looked at his mother,
As her eyes filled with many tears,
He knows that he's hurt her,
Being locked away in here.
His father is a just man,
Someone he didn't know,
So he never really missed him,
Somethings he just out grown.
When he stopped to think,
And take a look at his life,
He's at the appropriate age,
Where he should have a wife.
But instead he is here,
Being judged and treated unfair,
Feeling so much remorse,
But they think he doesn't care.
No one knows how he feels,
They look at him with rage,
That's why he feels like an animal,
Locked away in a steel cage.

Left All Alone

Left all alone, sometimes with a concrete bed
Lying on the gravel, many times not fed
The roaring of my bowels, as my tummy begins to ache
Wondering why me, was I the mistake
Physically I am here, but mentally I'm gone
This what it feels, when you're left all alone
My face is filthy, and my body smells bad
My clothes are ripped, this was all I had
My shoes have no soles, and my feet often bleed
My mouth full of sores, covered in disease
My throat is so dry, like a noose so tight
It feels like I'm strangling, throughout the cold night
As I lay on my back, and look at the sky
I'm begin to feel sad, as I begin to cry
My family tried to warn me, I had nothing to say
So I just learned things, the hard way
It was my fault, I left a perfectly good home
That's why I'm homeless, and left all alone

Life's Questions

What is love without struggle?
What is life without pain?
What are emotions if not shared?
What is failure with nothing to gain?
These are questions in life,
Through decisions I've made,
Although all may not be right,
I have survived just the same.
The struggles that I've had,
Were through my greatest fear,
To have given love to someone,
Who doesn't really care?
But that was a valued lesson,
Which I had to learn,
In order to give love,
It's something you have to earn.

Paper and Ink

Before I started writing,
This paper was completely blank,
Like a vault with no money,
Useless inside the bank.
As words began to form,
Developing inside my head,
I just kept repeating the line,
Then listened to what I said.
The more I kept hearing it,
Intuitively I began to think,
That's when I transcribed the words,
To paper with black ink.
I stopped to look at this artwork,
I created inside my mind,
Outwardly expressing myself,
In each and every line.
With emotions so strong,
Lifting off the page,
The words are being trapped,
Inside your mind like a cage.
Your mind is so focused,
And your heart is focused too,
We've become trapped inside the page,
Now what do we do?

The Puzzle of Life

Life is like a puzzle,
Unpredictable all the time,
When you open the box,
Who knows what you'll find.
As the pieces are scattered,
Some may reveal a clue,
The more pieces you have,
The more challenging it becomes too.
You realize this is too much,
You need someone to help,
This task would be too difficult,
To take on by yourself.
What if you knew someone?
Who knew what to do?
Who is willing to help?
Would you allow them to help you?

Tread Softly

No matter what is done,
We're being watched every day,
So we have to very careful,
In selecting the words we say.
Some people have the tendency,
While talking in the house,
To listen in on a conversation,
In order to run their mouths.
I kind of feel some tension,
There's something that I detect,
It only seems to happen to me,
It's definitely a lack of respect.
I can look over many things,
But some I just won't do,
I know you see what I see,
It has never happens to you.
I'm being very patient,
I've looked over so much stuff,
I can't take it anymore,
Enough is enough.

Dear Son

Dear Son,
When I was a little boy,
No different than you,
I looked forward to playing,
Just as much as you do.
We would run in the house,
And throw the ball outside,
I could hear you laughing,
When you were trying to hide.
We played video games,
We use to go to the park,
Throwing rocks in the pond,
Until it was nearly dark.
We use to watch television,
We use to play basketball,
We played in the house,
We nearly did it all.
Although you're not here,
I wish you could see,
How much I miss you,
And what you mean to me.

A Father's Love

Why do I feel the pain and agony each day?
When you don't care, to hear what I have to say
Why do you feel, that it's all about you?
When there's someone else, hurting as much as you
You can be so cold; and stubborn at times
It causes me to wonder, what's really on your mind?
You see, I may not have been
Everything you wanted me to be
But who is really at fault
For the expectations you have of me
Because I've tried to talk, but it's harder than I thought
You just want to be cruel, and claim it's my fault
Your eyes only visualize, what you want to see
But fail to acknowledge, the relationship between you and me
Or maybe I'm wrong, but I don't think so
If you would hear my side, then you would know
I refuse to chase you, so I'll let you be
Because being treated like this, isn't fair to me
You are my child, and that will never change
Remember it's my blood, which flows through your veins
It's my love that keeps me loving you, unconditionally and strong
Until the end of time, my love will continue on
You may not ever see this, but I don't know why
Because each day I open my eyes
In my heart, I continue to try
And I do all this and why
Because it's you I'm thinking of
To show the true meaning, of your father's love

Dear Brother

Dear Brother,
I know we haven't talked much,
Since daddy passed away,
I guess we both didn't have,
That much too really say.
I know you may be hurt,
I believe this to be true,
You have that strong exterior,
The pain won't pass through.
When I looked in your eyes,
There was something I could see,
The pain that they showed,
You do hurt like me.
You've handle things differently,
You've never shed a tear,
Through the time I've known you,
It's been several years.
We both are getting older,
We should be more brotherly,
If our father was here now,
He would want that for you and me.

What I See

When I watch television,
Someone's dying every day,
I see them as they mourn,
And also as they pray.
I see so much aggression,
And the consumption of greed,
We have so much going on,
The last thing that we need.
I see hopeless violence,
Imposed on our humanity,
People taking the lives of others,
This is what I see.

Mom

She loves with her heart,
And with all of her soul,
Some would say her heart,
Was made of pure gold.
She loves with compassion,
And so endlessly,
That's why a mother's love,
Is so important to me.
Her love is so thoughtful,
I think of her all the time,
No matter how far or near,
She's constantly on my mind.
Now that I'm older,
I really do understand,
It's hard for her to let go,
Because I am a grown man.

Why I Love to Write

I write because I want to express,
Myself in a different way,
My mind often feels trapped,
Doing it the conventional way.
With this type of outlet,
My conflict lies within,
Sometimes talking to another person,
It's not the same writing with paper and pen.
For these items don't judge,
Nor look at me in a weird way,
They are not opinionated,
For things that I might say.
This is also private,
I can read over it many times,
I can recall to myself,
The thought that was on my mind.
I write because I have emotions,
That sometimes I can't reveal,
Especially when I'm hurt,
Sometimes I just need to chill.
This is how I express my feelings,
Some many think it's not right,
This is my very reason,
Why I love to write.

A Strong Woman

You inspire me to be great,
When I think I'm just okay,
I can see your confidence in me,
Getting stronger each day.
Although I doubt myself,
Your commitment remains so strong,
Your faith solidifies me,
That's what keeps me going on.
Yes, I know we argue,
And at times we disagree,
But that doesn't cloud your judgment,
Of the potential inside of me.
And when you're not at your best,
I can see it in your eyes,
You're true to your word,
And always there by my side.
I've never seen anything,
Like this is my life,
I am so blessed and honored,
To call you my beloved wife.

A World in Crisis

Why must this continue?
Hasn't everyone seen enough?
These trials of injustice,
Disdainfully against us.
Are there any sadden hearts?
Are there any tears of pain?
Why can't we make peace?
Or better yet just abstain.
What motivates this attitude?
Is it right what we see?
Do you not understand the basis?
Of Dr. King's famous dream.
Someone's family is in mourning,
And no one can answer why,
There is no justification,
Why someone had to die.
We have to understand,
We must correct what's wrong,
If we continue to ignore it,
Our generation will soon be gone.

Because of You

Because of you,
I'm proud to be me,
I can look in the mirror,
Be proud of what I see.
Because of you,
I've accomplished much more,
More than I've ever,
Had done before.
Because of you,
I am so strong,
To have enough sense,
To know when I'm wrong.

Big Brother/Big Sister

I've always wanted a sibling,
Someone I could talk too,
A special big brother or sister,
Someone just like you.
He or she would guide me,
And help me along the way,
Someone to love and cherish,
Someone I could hug each day.
Someone who could help me,
To teach me to read and write,
Someone to help me with my prayers,
Before I go to bed at night.
Someone to go to the movies,
That would continue to watch after me,
This is truly my idea of,
What a big brother or sister should be.

Having Endurance

I've witnessed many things,
Through the evolution of time,
I've seen forms of discrimination,
Through decades of senseless crimes.
I've witnessed painful acts,
That has been done to another,
I've seen a joyous celebration,
A creation of love to a mother.
I've witnessed disappointment,
When things sometimes go wrong,
I've been blessed with determination,
That keeps me so strong.
I've experienced difficult times,
Which haven't been so nice?
But it has happened to us all,
That's just a part of life.
I've experienced great sadness,
Sometimes with much despair,
At times it felt too painful,
Much more than I can bear.
I've experienced all these things,
Just so I can say,
No matter how bad they are,
I thank Lord for another day.

Remember Me

I want to be remembered
As a kind and gentle soul,
The one who brought so much laughter?
To everyone he knows.
I want to be remembered,
As a true friend,
The one who stood by you,
Until the very end.
I want to be remembered,
How I forgave you,
Because that is what the Lord,
Would want me to do,
And if I can't be remembered,
For whatever reason there is,
My legacy will live on,
Through all of my kids.
And if I am forgotten,
That will be just fine,
We all must have some peace,
Deep within our minds.
And if I'm ever thought of,
Don't shed a tear for me,
Because I will be home,
The place I ought to be.

Survival

Through the struggles and troubles,
Commitments and lies
She fights for what's right,
As she continues to survive
In a cold, lonely place,
That often bares no face;
The reality of it all,
It breaths of disgrace
She does what she can,
Without the assistance of a man,
To set the example;
So her children could understand
No one owes you a thing,
No matter what you think,
Even if you are wearing a wedding ring
Keep your head up high;
And if they question you,
Here's your reply.
At times I may be alone,
But I have to be strong,
Because my foundation is considered,
To be my strongest backbone.

My Greatest Moment

When I was in summer league,
It was my turn at bat,
I was afraid of disappointing you,
And I didn't want to do that.
I would walk up to the plate,
Then turned to look at you,
You nod your head and clapped,
To see what I could do.
Now I was at the plate,
The umpire screamed play ball,
The pitcher began to wind up,
This first pitch was a ball.
I stepped out the batter's box,
To take another look,
The location of the first pitch,
The one which I just took.
The pitcher got the signal,
He finally delivered a strike,
The pitch looked good to me,
And I swung with all my might.
I connected and hit the ball,
And as it sailed high that day,
It went over the fence in left field,
As I watched it flew away.
I was so overjoyed,
I marveled at what I've done,
I can't actually believe it,
My very first homerun.

A Woman's Unconditional Love

When I didn't have a job,
Or a dime to my name,
You were there for me,
You didn't act ashamed.
And when I was upset,
And I took it out on you,
You stuck by my side,
It was you that helped me through.
And when I was sick,
And wasn't at my best,
It was you once more,
To help put my mind at rest.
When I didn't apologize,
For what I put you through,
Your actions never changed,
You did what you had to do.
And when I hurt your feelings,
You kept your head up high,
You didn't try to get even,
Even though I made you cry.
You loved me unconditionally,
And I believed this to be true,
You never abandoned me,
Or did what I did to you.

Foundation of Life

Before you commence to build, you must understand the situation
So when you start from the bottom, you must have a strong foundation
Once construction begins, you must monitor every link
Because one may seem so small, it could be stronger than you think
The principle applies to life, relationships, business, and all
Without a strong foundation, your building will soon fall
The trusses must be distributed, evenly and all around
The beams must be strong, and securely sound
The most important aspect, is caring for yourself
Don't ever sacrifice your heart, for someone else
Don't try to change anyone, that doesn't want the same
If they want a better life, then allow them to change
So if you all are meant to be, you all can try again
But try a different approach, and start off being friends

In the Name of Love

My life has evolved,
Through generations and time,
I've had many thoughts,
To come across my mind.
I have done many things,
Which some I'm not proud of,
My actions were justified,
In the name of love.
My life has changed,
And I recognized the signs,
I've gotten much older,
It was only a matter of time.
And to stay motivated,
Sometimes it wasn't enough,
But I still did it,
In the name of love.
My life is much happier,
Now that I have you,
I'm filled with joy,
Each time I see you.
My life is so joyous,
And now drama free,
This is how I know,
That you're the right one for me.
If I had to do it all again,
You know what I'll do,
I will continue to give my love,
My heart and soul to you.

Painful Moments

Even though I'm hurting,
I'm going to be fine,
I need to get myself together,
It's going to take some time.
But as I begin to heal,
I wanted you to know,
The things you've put me through,
They hurt me and you know.
Remember I'm strong,
I can live without you,
I did it once before,
This is what mature adults do.
I know there's a God,
He's been by my side,
He holds me in His arms,
He keeps me safe at night.
I have no hard feelings,
I have to let you be,
I'm not doing this for you,
I'm doing it more for me.

Life Experiences

I hate feeling this way, because it's not me
Often times I can't stand, the sight I often see
Or is it just the people, I'm surrounded by everyday
Or is it the things, which these people say
They say words don't hurt, but I strongly disagree
I can't tell you how to feel, nor can you tell me
Emotions run deep, just as do our thoughts
We act out on impulse, as most of us are taught
There's no right or wrong, it's just how it is
It hasn't changed in a while, since we were little kids
Trying to cope with it, can be challenging in itself
When you feel all alone, just you and no one else
Some people find it easy, just to walk away
But I'm much different; I want to handle it that day
But others are not responsive, as the way I may be
And that is the difference, between you and me
You may never know, what someone's going through
On that particular day, they may lash out at you
It's not personal, so watch what you say
You don't know how, it's going to affect that person's day
If we all could be mindful, things wouldn't be the same
And that's what I'm striving, for that type of change

Emotions

I often find myself,
Moving in slow motion,
For no particular reason,
Without any emotion.
My mind is often wondering,
Without a destination or trace,
Wandering through this world,
In an unfamiliar place.
I'm surrounded by silence,
With the absence of a crowd,
Even though I'm alone,
At times that seems too loud.
I can't figure it out,
And I don't know why,
It's like a feeling of pain,
For some reason I can't cry.
I know it sounds confusing,
Or even crazy at times,
It's so difficult to explain,
The imagery within my mind.
If emotions were words,
And if words could think,
What would they say?
If those words could speak?

My Gift

When I acknowledge a talent,
That I didn't have before,
I work harder to exploit it,
I try to hone my skill much more.
I start by understanding,
The gift that was given to me,
To use it for the sole purpose,
Of why the Lord gave it to me.
It was meant to be shared,
To touch the life of someone,
Who may be angry or depressed?
Who may think their life is done.
A talent can be used,
To discourage much despair,
By allowing your thoughts to flow,
To resonate anywhere.
We all possess a talent,
That we're not familiar with,
We have an obligation,
To find and hone your gift.

Dear Dad

Dear Dad,
I know I never told you, I thought about it each day
To tell you that I love you, in some kind of manly way
But somehow I forgot, I knew I would try again
Not only you're my father, I view you as a friend
I thought of you as a hero, you were one of a kind
You were a positive influence, thank you for taking the time
I saw you as a drill instructor, you were hard on me
You gave a glimpse, of what a man is supposed to be
Each time I came home, I expected to see you
I took those things for granted, as children often do
Although it took some time, now I really see
My dad wasn't just a dad; he was the greatest to me

Treasures of the Heart

Diamonds, silver, and gold,
Can be easily viewed as treasure,
Due to their elusive properties,
That renders many pleasures.
It could be the value,
Or it could be the shine,
Or maybe it's the fascination,
That sparks curiosity into the mind.
But there's another treasure,
That's been a blessing for a while,
That carries a benevolent feeling,
And always brings a smile.
It derives from the heart,
It also comforts the mind,
It delivers a wonderful feeling,
Each and every time.
It could be shared by many,
Or it could just be two,
That's what makes it so special,
Because I feel this way about you.

Deeply Thinking

Deeply thinking to me,
Is something that's true?
It's a part of yourself,
No one knows but you.
It's not easily shared,
It's not something you can hide,
It's a feeling of emotions,
Where deep thoughts reside.
The challenging part,
Is when it's revealed?
You must enjoy the moment,
The rush of the thrill.
Deeply thinking to me,
Place challenges on you,
To do much better than before,
Then you're accustom too.
It pushes you to the limit,
It takes up your time,
Until you reveal the truth,
Of what's really on your mind.
So please open you heart,
If you think you will see,
This is what I believe,
Deeply thinking is to me.

Printed in the United States
By Bookmasters